WO...
CO...
AN...
...ICS

KID ENGINEER

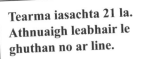
WAYLAND
www.waylandbooks.co.uk

First published in Great Britain in 2020 by Wayland

Copyright © Hodder and Stoughton, 2020

Produced for Wayland by
White-Thomson Publishing Ltd
www.wtpub.co.uk

All rights reserved
ISBN: 978 1 5263 1319 5 (HB)
978 1 5263 1320 1 (PB)

MIX
Paper from
responsible sources
FSC® C104740

Credits
Editor: Sonya Newland
Illustrator: Diego Vaisberg
Designer: Clare Nicholas

Every attempt has been made to clear copyright. Should there be any
inadvertent omission please apply to the publisher for rectification.

Printed in China

Wayland
An imprint of
Hachette Children's Group
Part of The Watts Publishing Group
Carmelite House
50 Victoria Embankment
London EC4Y 0DZ

An Hachette UK Company
www.hachette.co.uk
www.hachettechildrens.co.uk

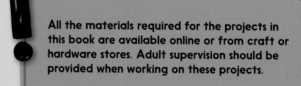

All the materials required for the projects in
this book are available online or from craft or
hardware stores. Adult supervision should be
provided when working on these projects.

CONTENTS

RISE OF THE MACHINES

Engineers come up with ideas to solve problems. They invent, design, develop and build all sorts of things, from smartphones and satnavs to skyscrapers and spacecraft. Some engineers work with computers and robotics.

What are computers?

Look around you – what do you see? A laptop and mobile phone? A games console or a smart TV? These are all types of computer or computer-powered device. A computer is a machine that stores and processes information. To carry out different operations, a computer follows instructions given to it through a program.

1822 Charles Babbage designs the first mechanical computer.

1840s Ada Lovelace writes the first algorithm (see pages 14–15) for Babbage's 'Analytical Engine'.

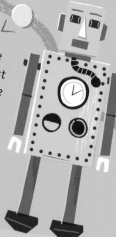

1932 The first wind-up robot toy, the Lilliput, is made in Japan.

1936 Alan Turing designs the 'universal machine' (see page 5).

1946 ENIAC is the first electronic digital computer

1954 George Devol and Joe Engelberger invent the first programmable robotic arm.

1958 Jack Kilby and Robert Noyce invent the computer chip.

What is robotics?

Machines that do work are called robots. They are usually powered by computer chips and have sensors that help them respond to their environment. Robotics is the science of designing and building robots.

Careers for engineers!

Computer engineers design and test all the different parts of a computer. They also come up with ideas for new computer technology. Robotics engineers identify where a machine could do a job or make life easier. Then they design and build a robot to fulfil that need.

Special skills

Computer and robotics engineers need to have a good understanding of maths and science. They must be creative, curious and brilliant problem-solvers. They also have to keep up to date with all the latest technology!

SORTED!

The first modern, working computer was devised by British mathematician Alan Turing in 1936. He suggested the idea of a 'universal machine' that could work out any computable problem. During the Second World War (1939–45), Turing created a machine that could crack enemy codes. After the war, Turing worked at Manchester University, where the first stored-program computer was built in 1948, based on his universal machine.

2000 Honda creates the humanoid robot ASIMO.

2007 Apple launches the iPhone smartphone, using computer technology.

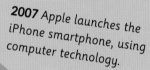

1999 Sony launches AIBO, a robotic dog that can learn things and communicate.

1991 The first laptop computer goes on sale.

1990 Tim Berners-Lee develops HTML, a computer language that allows pages to be displayed on the internet.

2020 NASA launches a new Mars mission with the robotic Mars 2020 rover.

1963 Douglas Engelbart invents the computer mouse.

HARDWARE AND SOFTWARE

Today, computers are more complex and powerful than ever. But there are still two key components that engineers have to design and build: hardware and software. Hardware is all the physical parts of a computer. Software is any program that gives a computer the instructions it needs to work.

Hardware basics

Hardware engineers design everything you can see that is part of a computer. They also create some things you can't see!

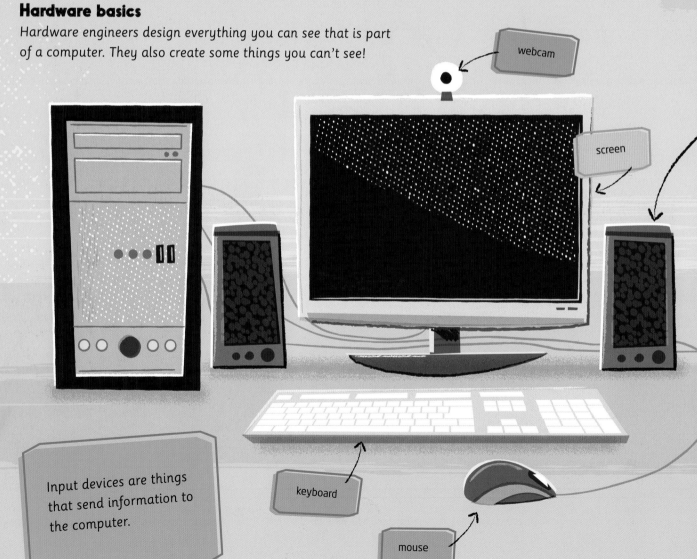

webcam

screen

Input devices are things that send information to the computer.

keyboard

mouse

Processing

Processing devices run calculations to make the computer work. The main piece of processing hardware is the central processing unit (CPU). Designing processors is a special engineering skill. Processor designers have to understand how the parts of a processor are put together to work in a particular way.

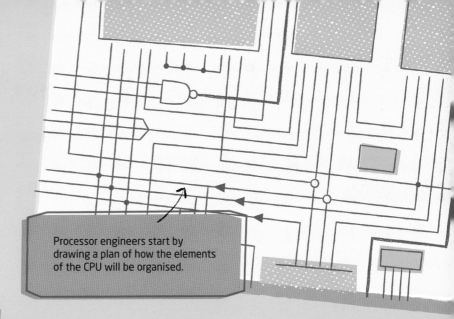

Processor engineers start by drawing a plan of how the elements of the CPU will be organised.

Output devices are things that show information to the user.

speakers

printer

Software engineering

Software engineers write programs for computers. First, the engineers find out what the computer needs to do, such as run a web browser or a video game. Then they design a program that will give the computer the instructions it needs to perform this task.

SORTED!

Grace Hopper (1906–92) was one of the first computer engineers. She helped develop the computer UNIVAC and the programming language COBOL. One day she was working on a computer when a moth got inside the machine. After that, Hopper used the word 'bug' to describe when a computer failed. We still use this expression today.

Storage

Storage is hardware that holds information. Storage devices might store information permanently (such as the hard drive) or just temporarily (such as RAM).

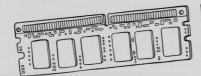

RAM stands for **Random Access Memory**. RAM is a computer's main memory system. It **stores information** only while the computer is working with it.

YOU'RE THE ENGINEER: BINARY BEADS

Computers store information using a system called binary. Binary means there are only two options. For example, binary numbers are 0 and 1. Start work as a software engineer by getting to grips with binary code using beads.

You will need
A pencil and paper
Beads in two different colours, plus white beads
A piece of string

1 Look at the binary code for the alphabet. We have used blue and yellow here, but the binary options could be any two colours.

Letter	Binary
A	
B	
C	
D	
E	
F	
G	
H	
I	
J	
K	
L	
M	

Letter	Binary
N	
O	
P	
Q	
R	
S	
T	
U	
V	
W	
X	
Y	
Z	

2 Find the first letter of your name and copy out the two groups of bits (squares) that make up that letter on your piece of paper.

3 Now find the second letter of your name and copy the code on to your paper. Repeat until you have the binary pattern for your whole name.

4 Take one colour of beads and place them on all the bits of the first colour. Take the second colour of beads and place them on the other bits. (What name have we made here?)

5 At the end of each line representing a letter, place a white bead. This is called a delimiter. It marks the space between letters.

6 Thread the beads on to the string in the correct order, with a delimiter between each letter, to create a necklace or bracelet that spells your name in binary.

TEST IT!

You can use anything that appears in two forms to write in binary code. Write some simple statements, then challenge a friend to write them in binary using:

shapes (a circle and a triangle)

coins (heads and tails)

vegetables (peas and carrot slices).

PRINTED CIRCUIT BOARDS

Every computer contains a printed circuit board (PCB). Before building a PCB, hardware engineers map out the board in a diagram called a schematic. They use symbols to show where different components will go.

Bits of the board

A PCB contains an electrical circuit. This is a bit like the ones you might have created in science, using wires, batteries and light bulbs. In a computer, the circuit is much smaller and it has a lot more parts! It connects many different components to make the computer work.

Capacitors store electrical charge.

POWER

The board, or 'card', is made of a non-conducting material such as plastic or fibreglass. This ensures that electricity will only flow through the circuit, not the board.

Electrical components are connected to the board using a metal called solder.

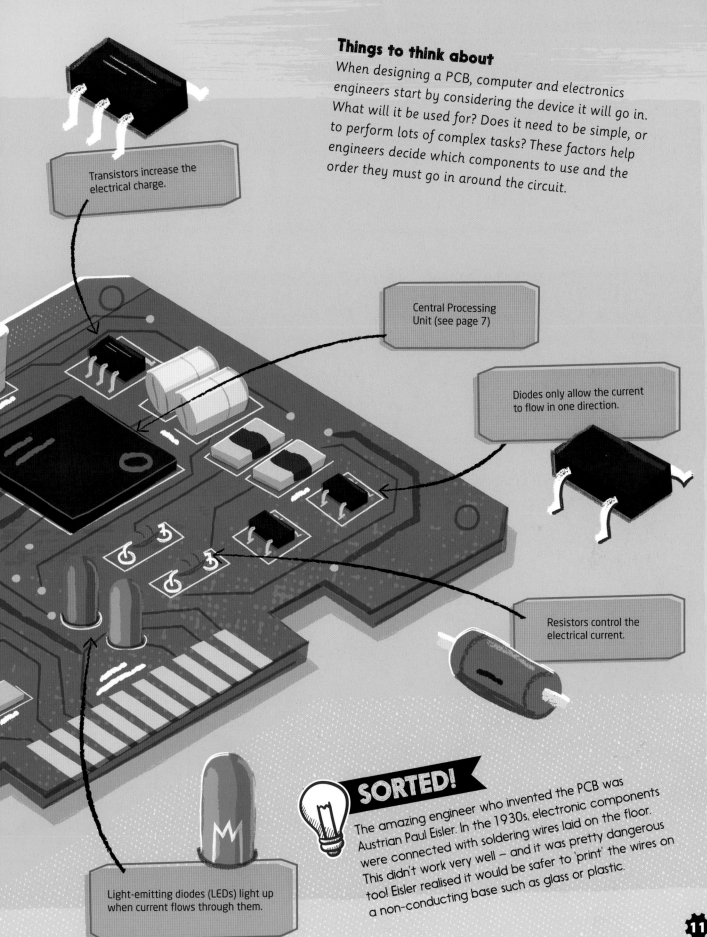

Transistors increase the electrical charge.

Things to think about

When designing a PCB, computer and electronics engineers start by considering the device it will go in. What will it be used for? Does it need to be simple, or to perform lots of complex tasks? These factors help engineers decide which components to use and the order they must go in around the circuit.

Central Processing Unit (see page 7)

Diodes only allow the current to flow in one direction.

Resistors control the electrical current.

Light-emitting diodes (LEDs) light up when current flows through them.

SORTED!

The amazing engineer who invented the PCB was Austrian Paul Eisler. In the 1930s, electronic components were connected with soldering wires laid on the floor. This didn't work very well – and it was pretty dangerous too! Eisler realised it would be safer to 'print' the wires on a non-conducting base such as glass or plastic.

BIG DATA

What's the BIGGEST job you can do in the field of computer science? A big data engineer!

What is big data?

Big data is basically *loads* of information. Think of the names of everyone in your class, then year, then school. Then think of their age, eye colour, favourite TV show... You can't store all that information, but a computer can.

Where does it come from?

Big data is gathered from lots of different sources. Every time you 'like' a post, watch a video or click on a link on social media, that information is stored.

Interpreting information

All those likes and links can tell a company if you enjoy hip-hop music or tennis or video games – or all of them! Once they have that information, it can be used to create a dataset. A dataset is a collection of related pieces of information that a computer can read and interpret. For example, a dataset might have information about all the people on a social media site who like tennis. Analysing that information could reveal what other shared interests these people have.

Whenever you buy something, computers record what you bought, where you bought it, how much you paid, what else you bought at the same time – and a lot more.

Engineering big data

Some big data engineers come up with systems for storing big data. This could be hardware or software. Others interpret the data to find patterns in the information. Those patterns can be used in thousands of different ways.

BIG DATA APPLICATIONS

Financial:
Big data helps banks understand patterns in how people spend and save their money.

Healthcare:
Big data can show patterns in illnesses and can be used to stop the spread of disease.

Retail:
Real-world and online shops can improve sales by learning more about people's buying patterns.

Energy:
Energy companies can analyse how people use renewable and non-renewable resources.

Telecommunications:
Big data can tell phone companies about the location and movement of their users and the reliability and popularity of their services.

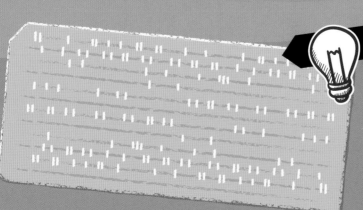

SORTED!

The first computers could not store data. To solve this problem, American engineer Herman Hollerith (1860–1929) used a system of punched cards. Holes were punched in columns on a card. Each column represented one character and one card was used for each line of code.

AMAZING ALGORITHMS

Computers are able to collect data and solve problems thanks to algorithms. These are special instructions for how to complete a task. They are designed and written by algorithm engineers, a type of software engineer.

Algorithms everywhere

Algorithms might sound complicated, but in fact you use them every day. An algorithm is simply a set of step-by-step instructions for completing a task. Every time you brush your teeth, phone a friend or make a cup of tea, you're using an algorithm.

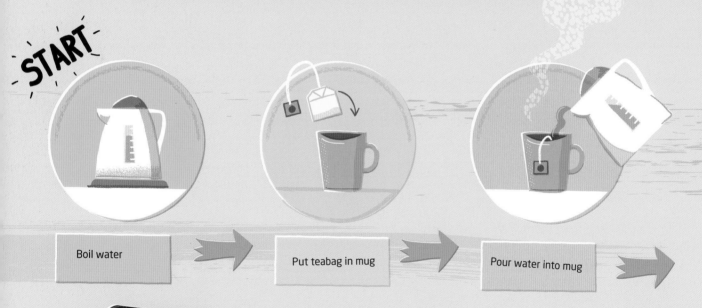

START

| Boil water | → | Put teabag in mug | → | Pour water into mug | → |

Accuracy and efficiency

Algorithm engineers have to think about two key things. First, the algorithm has to solve the problem. Second, it has to do so in the most efficient way. An algorithm designed to help people find a route from Paris to Berlin is no good if it takes travellers via London!

Types of algorithm

Linear algorithms show a single route to the outcome. However, most tasks require some decision-making. These are branching algorithms. For example, some people might take sugar in their tea. To allow for this, an engineer would need to program a 'branch' that includes a step for adding sugar.

Loops and conditionals

To allow users to interact with the algorithm and make decisions, engineers use conditional statements and loops. A conditional statement allows for different steps depending on the user's requirements, such as finding out if someone takes sugar in their tea. The instruction is often in the form 'If... then...'. A loop is a step that is repeated until a condition is met. It may be based on a 'yes/no' question, such as asking if the kettle is boiling.

STOP

Leave for one minute → Remove teabag → Add milk → Stir

SORTED!

In 1996, Google founders Larry Page and Sergey Brin were looking for a way to sort search results. They wanted the best websites to appear first. So, they created an algorithm called PageRank. PageRank counted the number of links that each website relevant to the search had and gave each website a value between 0 and 10. The algorithm sorted the results so that the websites with the highest values came out on top.

YOU'RE THE ENGINEER: UNDERSTANDING ALGORITHMS

Writing an algorithm involves figuring out every single thing you need to do. Leave something out, and the program won't work. Practise your algorithm engineering skills by designing and building a cup tower.

You will need

Nine paper cups
Two blank pieces of
    A4 paper
A pencil
The cup placement
    key (right)

Key

Starter cup

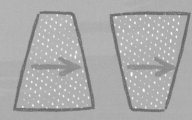

Put a cup on the left

Put a cup on top

Put a cup on the right

1 On the first piece of A4 paper, design a structure of stacked cups. Try to use all nine cups. You can have as many cups as you like on each layer. They can be the right way up or upside down.

2 On the second piece of A4 paper, draw a grid five squares high and six squares wide.

3 In the grid, draw the algorithm to build your cup structure. Use the key on page 16 to mark how the cups should be placed.

4 Now, following your algorithm, build your cup structure. Be careful to follow the steps exactly as you have drawn them in the grid. Does your algorithm work? If not, go back to the grid and change the order of the steps.

5 Test your finished algorithm on a friend. Can they follow your steps to build the structure you designed?

TEST IT!

Remember, when dealing with algorithms, there may be more than one way to get the same result. Draw another grid. This time, pick a different starting position on the grid. Design a different algorithm that gives you the same cup structure.

HELPFUL ROBOTS

One of the great things about robots is that they can't get bored. That's why engineers usually design robots to help humans to do work, especially simple, repetitive tasks.

Factory favourites

Engineers first began building robots to work in factories. They designed different robots to do different tasks on a production line. Today, engineers plan out the shape, size and movement of their robots according to the tasks they need to do. Car factories are filled with robots welding, assembling, painting and testing cars!

Help around the house

Have you seen a vacuum cleaner that works on its own? What about a lawnmower you don't have to push? Robotics engineers often focus on designing and improving robots like these, which are becoming more and more popular around the home.

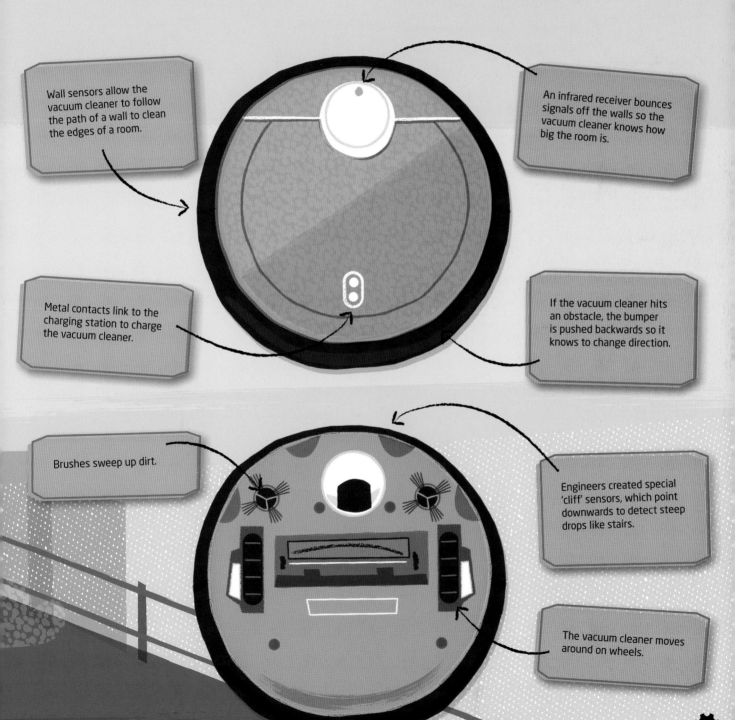

Wall sensors allow the vacuum cleaner to follow the path of a wall to clean the edges of a room.

An infrared receiver bounces signals off the walls so the vacuum cleaner knows how big the room is.

Metal contacts link to the charging station to charge the vacuum cleaner.

If the vacuum cleaner hits an obstacle, the bumper is pushed backwards so it knows to change direction.

Brushes sweep up dirt.

Engineers created special 'cliff' sensors, which point downwards to detect steep drops like stairs.

The vacuum cleaner moves around on wheels.

YOU'RE THE ENGINEER: BUILD A BRUSHBOT

Complex robots are powered by computer chips, but you can engineer a simple robot powered by a battery and motor.

You will need

A toothbrush
A 6-mm vibrating motor
A 3V battery
Double-sided sticky tape
Googly craft eyes

1 Press the toothbrush head against a hard surface until the bristles are splayed outwards.

2 Get an adult to cut the handle off the toothbrush so you just have the head. Cut a piece of the double-sided tape and stick it to the flat part of the toothbrush head.

3 Stick the vibrating motor on top of the tape. Put another piece of tape on the handle. Keep one wire in the air and place the other on the tape, with the exposed bit of the wire slightly raised.

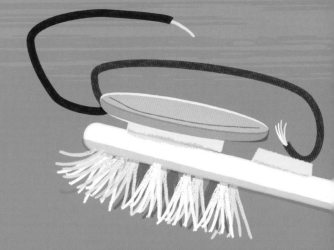

4 Put the battery, negative side down, over the wire on the tape. Make sure the battery is fully touching the wire.

5 Stick the googly eyes on the front to finish off your brushbot. Then it's time to watch your bot go! To activate it, position the top wire so that it's touching the top (positive) side of the battery. The bot should start moving.

TEST IT!

Build a second brushbot but this time don't splay the bristles first. Which brushbot do you think will be faster? Race them to find out. How could you give your brushbot 'sensors', so that it responds to its environment by moving away from obstacles?

WHERE HUMANS CAN'T GO

Humans are not suited for life in certain environments. We can't breathe in space or under water, for example. So, engineers have started designing and building robots that can explore space and deep beneath the oceans.

Roving Mars

The rovers were four special robots sent to Mars. They were cleverly designed to help NASA scientists find out more about the planet.

THE MARS ROVER CURIOSITY

Cameras take photographs of the landscape and send them back to Earth.

Antennae allow the rover to communicate with scientists on Earth.

Navigation cameras make sure the rover avoids obstacles.

Solar panels channel energy from the Sun to charge their lithium batteries.

A robotic arm (see page 23) collects soil samples and can even be used as a selfie stick!

Wide wheels help the rover move over rocks and sand.

Engineering issues

The Mars rovers included some incredible engineering. Software engineers designed programs to help the rovers navigate and to create maps of Mars. Hardware engineers had to design the vehicles so they could survive tough terrain, freezing temperatures and dust.

One motor in the 'elbow' allows the arm to fold up or out.

Motors in the 'shoulder' move the arm from side to side.

The Curiosity rover's robotic arm collected samples of rocks and soil from Mars's surface, which told scientists back on Earth a lot about the planet.

Two motors in the 'wrist' allow precise movements horizontally or vertically.

Delving deep

Unmanned underwater vehicles map and take photographs of the ocean bed. They have to be specially designed. Satellites can't penetrate under water so GPS doesn't work there. Engineers have developed software to help the vehicles navigate using acoustics, or sound.

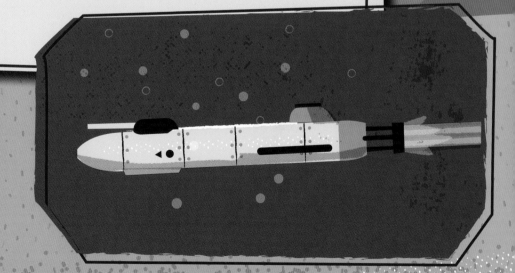

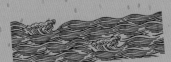
To withstand the **huge weight** of water, engineers build underwater vehicles out of **super-strong materials** such as titanium.

YOU'RE THE ENGINEER: ROBOTIC ARM

Many robots, including the Mars rovers, have 'arms'. Robotic arms are a lot like human arms, with joints that are moved by flexible parts. Become a robotics engineer and build your own robotic arm.

You will need

A large strip of strong
 cardboard (5 cm x 20 cm)
A smaller strip of cardboard
 (5 cm x 10 cm)
A brass split fastener
A drinking straw
1 m of string
Two large paper
 clips
Sticky tape
Scissors
A hole punch
A paper cup

1 Punch a hole in the corner of each strip of cardboard and join them with the split fastener.

2 Cut the straw into 2.5-cm pieces. Use the sticky tape to attach them lengthways to the long piece of cardboard. Keep one piece of straw for the small piece of cardboard and attach it in the same way.

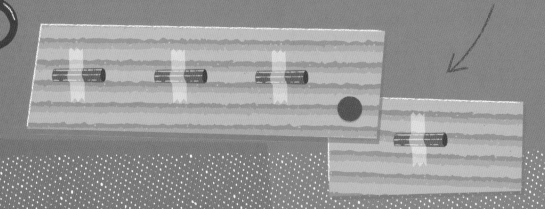

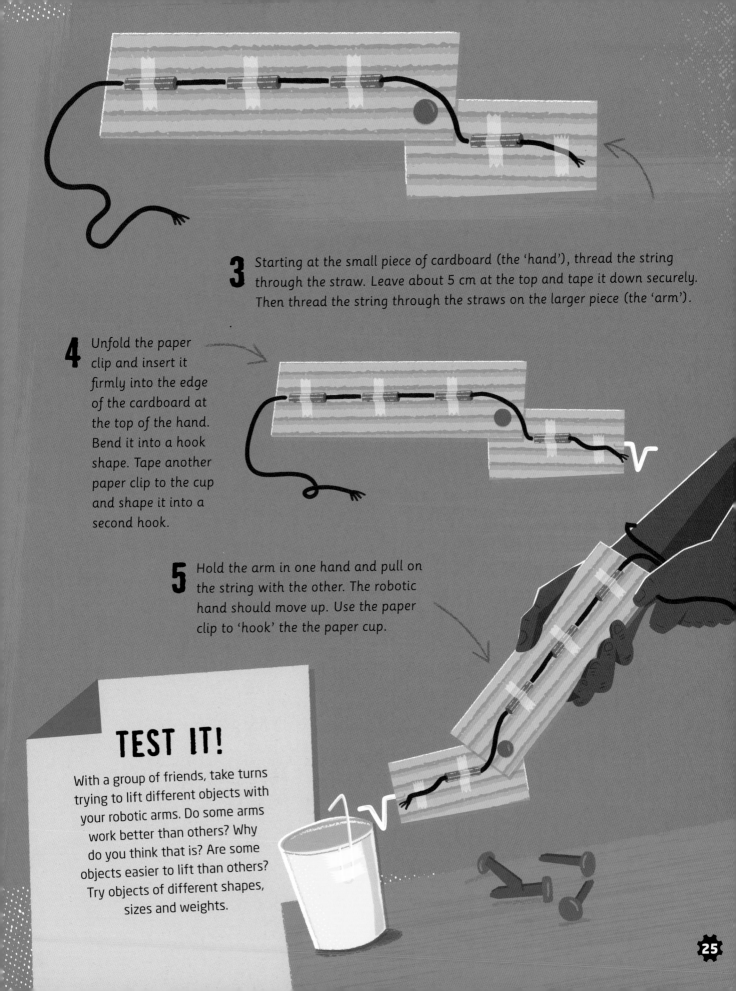

3 Starting at the small piece of cardboard (the 'hand'), thread the string through the straw. Leave about 5 cm at the top and tape it down securely. Then thread the string through the straws on the larger piece (the 'arm').

4 Unfold the paper clip and insert it firmly into the edge of the cardboard at the top of the hand. Bend it into a hook shape. Tape another paper clip to the cup and shape it into a second hook.

5 Hold the arm in one hand and pull on the string with the other. The robotic hand should move up. Use the paper clip to 'hook' the the paper cup.

TEST IT!

With a group of friends, take turns trying to lift different objects with your robotic arms. Do some arms work better than others? Why do you think that is? Are some objects easier to lift than others? Try objects of different shapes, sizes and weights.

ARTIFICIAL INTELLIGENCE

Some engineers are working on ways to make robots more like humans. They want to give them the ability to think and learn. This area of computers and robotics is called artificial intelligence (AI).

Inside the mind of a machine

Most computers and robots rely on human input. They work only if we tell them what to do. But engineers are starting to design 'intelligent computers'. These machines gain knowledge and skills through their own experiences, just like humans.

Strong AI is when machines have an intelligence very similar to humans. They are self-aware, which means that they can think, learn and perform tasks on their own.

Weak (or narrow) AI is when machines can perform a single task. They can improve at that task, but they cannot learn new tasks.

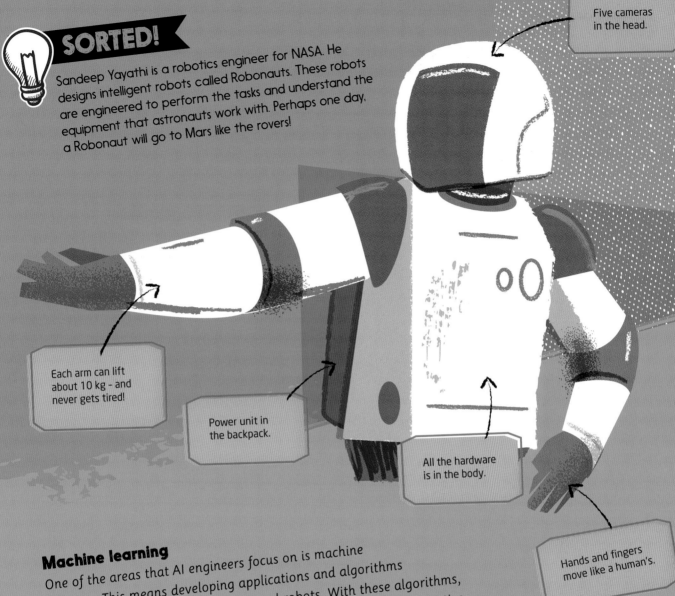

Sandeep Yayathi is a robotics engineer for NASA. He designs intelligent robots called Robonauts. These robots are engineered to perform the tasks and understand the equipment that astronauts work with. Perhaps one day, a Robonaut will go to Mars like the rovers!

Five cameras in the head.

Each arm can lift about 10 kg – and never gets tired!

Power unit in the backpack.

All the hardware is in the body.

Hands and fingers move like a human's.

Machine learning

One of the areas that AI engineers focus on is machine learning. This means developing applications and algorithms (see page 14) that train computers and robots. With these algorithms, machines get better at performing tasks through learning and practice.

All in the game

One of the earliest experiments with intelligent computers was 'Deep Blue'. This chess-playing 'supercomputer' was designed by the computer company IBM. It went up against world champion chess player Gary Kasparov in 1997 – and won.

IBM also developed the question-answering computer system Watson for the TV show *Jeopardy*. In this quiz, the questions are actually answers and the answers are given in the form of questions. Understanding language in this way is a very human skill!

WHAT DOES THE FUTURE HOLD?

Computing and robotics are already amazing areas of engineering. Every new idea opens up new opportunities. What engineering field of the future might you work in?

Smaller and smaller

Nanotechnology involves engineering on a very small scale. This may have a big effect on medicine. Engineers are developing nanobots – robots that are so tiny they could move around easily inside the human body. By targeting particular cells in the body, nanobots may one day help cure serious diseases.

Robots are already used in surgical procedures. Nanobots could go even further in treating medical conditions.

Bigger and bigger

Big data is getting bigger. More and more information is collected, stored and used. Big data engineers need to create hardware and software that can cope with all this information. They are also continually finding new ways to analyse and use it.

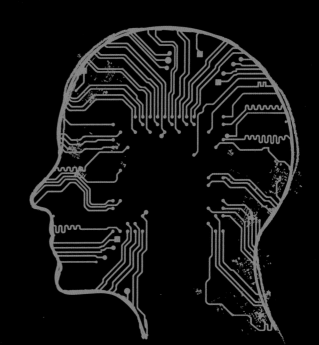

The car manufacturer Tesla is using AI engineering to develop 'thinking' algorithms. They intend to use this to build fully autonomous cars, which can drive without human input.

Smarter and smarter

AI engineers are working on new ways to 'teach' computers and robots. They are also designing hardware that could put this intelligence to thousands of different uses. For example, they are engineering devices that will respond to students' individual needs in the classroom. If you could teach a machine to do anything, what would it be?

SORTED!

Computer, software and data engineering are key to security and policing these days. Cyber crime investigators use the latest in software and data engineering to solve crimes. Forensics experts use amazing engineering to piece together evidence, such as specialist imaging equipment and facial-recognition software.

The **'Internet of Things'** is the way we now **describe** how **everything** in our world is **connected** via the internet, computers and everyday devices.

GLOSSARY

algorithm a set of steps that tell a computer what to do to achieve a task

binary a coding system that uses only the numbers 0 and 1 in different combinations

circuit a system of wires, batteries and other components that electricity flows around

code the 'language' that engineers use to program computers

current the flow of electricity round a circuit

delimeter a space at the end of a sequence of code

fibreglass a strong, light material made up of fine glass fibres

GPS global positioning system; a way of tracking where things are using satellites

humanoid describing something that looks and behaves like a human

infrared a type of radiation that can be used to send signals that cannot be seen by the human eye

nanotechnology the science, technology and engineering of tiny things

NASA National Aeronautics and Space Administration – the USA's space agency

non-renewable resources things that can't be reproduced and will run out

production line a system in factories where things are built

program a series of coded instructions that tell a computer what to do

RAM Random Access Memory; the main memory device in a computer, which stores information just while the computer is working with it

renewable resources resources that can be reproduced and will not run out

satnav a device that uses satellites to show your exact location

schematic a diagram of an electrical component such as a circuit board, showing where all the wires and other components go

sensor a device that detects and responds to physical objects

social media apps and websites that allow users to share content and interact

solder a soft metal that melts easily, used for joining other types of metal together

FURTHER INFORMATION

Books

A Robot World by Clive Gifford (Franklin Watts, 2019)
Computers (Adventures in STEAM) by Claudia Martin (Wayland, 2017)
Computing and Coding in the Real World (Get Ahead in Computing)
 by Clive Gifford (Wayland, 2017)
Robotics Engineering (Science Brain Builders) by Ed Sobery (Raintree, 2017)
Robots (Adventures in STEAM) by Izzi Howell (Wayland, 2017)
Robots (Code: STEM) by Max Wainewright (Wayland, 2019)

Websites

spaceplace.nasa.gov/mars-rovers/en/
Find out all about NASA's Mars rovers programme, and what it has planned
next for the red planet.

www.youtube.com/watch?v=P18EdAKuC1U
Watch IBM's intelligent computer Watson take on some of the human
champions of the quiz *Jeopardy*.

dcmp.org/media/9874-sandeep-yayathi-robotics-engineer
Sandeep Yayathi introduces one of his Robonauts and explains how
these robots may help in the future of space exploration.

The websites (URLs) included in this book were valid at the time of going to press.
However, it is possible that contents or addresses may have changed since the
publication of this book. No responsibility for any such changes can be accepted by
either the author or the publisher.

INDEX